RUSSIAN SUBMARINES

Guardians of the Motherland

An illustrated view

By Wayne Frey

A Cardinal production
Part One

ISBN 0-7414-3447-4

Published by:

INFI∞ITY
PUBLISHING.COM
1094 New DeHaven Street, Suite 100
West Conshohocken, PA 19428-2713
Info@buybooksontheweb.com
www.buybooksontheweb.com
Toll-free (877) BUY BOOK
Local Phone (610) 941-9999
Fax (610) 941-9959

Printed in the United States of America

Printed on Recycled Paper

Published July 2006

"The sea man does not have the easy way; there is also no difficult way.
There is only one way. Famous!"

Admiral Nahimov

For Sergey

Contents

Prologue

The reader will notice that many of the photographs are older, lesser quality, black and white pictures. A few are less clear because they were taken from videos. While today's world has easy to carry digital cameras that take outstanding pictures, these are very unique in their own way.

It is the purpose of this book to illustrate details of the submarines shown. Dry dock photographs are the ideal for this purpose. In addition, I am adding some newer pictures that are my favorites.

Many of these took years to obtain, with hundreds of hours research. It is a passion I do enjoy, being the student of Russian submarines. It has taken me around the world several times. I have met some wonderful people, a fascinating culture, and some very interesting places. I will continue my pursuits and will produce another book on different classes of Russian submarines. I also have some outstanding video I will be releasing soon.

I wish to thank the websites that helped, submarina.org, and deepstorm.ru. Hartmut Ehlers, for providing a wealth of information of new information about the Beluga, and Don Meadows for his support.

I would like to thank the St. Petersburg Submarine Club, in St. Petersburg Russia, for helping the orphans and widows of submariners still at sea. And, for being a focal point of the men that served for their motherland on submarines. A true, international Brotherhood of the Fin, of which I am a member.

The Subcommittee and Sub pirates are both groups of fine submarine enthusiasts that helped beyond words. I encourage anyone interested to go to the websites and join in.

The incomparable Mr. Merrimen, Steve Sneill, Antoine, and many others, that I am fortunate to count as friends and supporters.

I also wish to sincerely thank those outside and inside of Russia, who will remain anonymous for their betterment.

My wish is that the reader discovers and enjoys the contents of these pages. I certainly enjoyed bringing them to this book.

I am always interested in new photographs. If you have something not common to the internet or other books, please contact me at: gatorfrey@hotmail.com

Some of these pictures that follow were readily available. Some, I obtained permission from inside Russia. The exceptional ones, I bought and own outright. In publishing this book, all measures have been taken to ensure that ALL contents are copyrighted and legally the property of Cardinal Productions. They are not to be reprinted, distributed by any means, copied, photocopied, or otherwise used without my expressed written consent.

Enjoy!
Wayne Frey

Ahead of it's time, the Alfa 705

K123. The first 705 K version.

K123 on the left.
The difference in height out of the waterline is characteristic to the large reserve buoyancy that
all the double hull Russian submarines carry.

Zapadnaya Lista.
A special support base designed to support the Alfa. Here, the steam could keep the lead reactors at temperature, or the reactor had to be left running. If the reactor dropped below critical temperature and froze, it would have to be removed and disposed.

Again, K123. Here one sees the periscope and antenna array behind the cockpit escape capsule.

Five of the six operational Alfas that were built. A seventh had begun construction, but was never completed.

An Alfa dockside.

Bow section of an Alfa dockside

Dockside port view of the Alfa sail

Close view of the shutter doors on the outer hull, or "easy case" as the Russians refer to it. The "hard case" is the inner pressure hull itself.

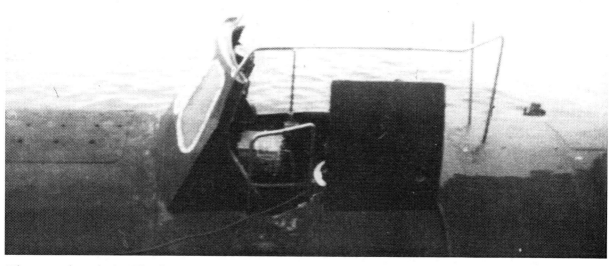

The actual cockpit. The frame going from the windscreen to the hull is for a canvas cover for the Severe weather frequently encountered in the Barents Sea.

Just aft of the sail, the marker buoy location is visible. Immediately behind this is a tight seam that is seen. That is the leading edge of the cover that is over the nuclear reactor.

Topside farther to the stern. Bollards, or devices that rise up for securing at port, are seen.

Rear forward opening hatch at the stern. Also shown are simple, robust tie down points that are laying flush with the hull at the moment. Note also the safety track. One secures himself by lanyard to this when topside at sea to prevent being lost overboard.

Alfa upper rudder. The V-shaped cut in the rudder is for navigation light

An Alfa in dry dock for decommissioning.
Note the vortex attenuator on the screw hub. It is one of many characteristics found
on the Alfa that can be seen on most subsequent nuclear boats of the Russian Navy.
Body of revolution design is clear.

The easy case cover for the reactor seen on the ground.

The upper rudder and stern section. Note the straight taper instead of the suspected hogner type.

The bow section.

From the stern looking forward. Safety track is clearly visible to the left.

Starboard view of the graceful hull. The two larger rectangular ports seen slightly above the rest are for the exhaust of the reactor seawater. The smooth bulge just above the ice is the intake.

Starboard front quarter photograph

The business end of an Alfa

11

Torpedo doors can be seen despite wear from service.
Also, not visible, the Alfa does have staggered bow planes. They are just off the centerline and offset by the thickness of the opposing plane. This was done solely due to size constraints.

A closer look at the bow.
Bow planes are just behind the two side shutters and at the midline.

Begin a portside view

Lead hatch removed on the sail.
Note it is low and slightly offset to port. Also instrumentation cover is removed.

The escape module has been removed.
The Soviet Star is seen painted on the sail.

The symmetrical hatch also open here.
Antenna hatches are removed and some grillwork can be seen here.

Safety track begins at the base of the hatch and goes back to the rear hatch ahead of the rudder.

Under the reactor "easy case" cover, a row of cylinders can be seen. These are represented in some internal illustrations of the Alfa.

Good detail here. Grill above and behind the rear hatch. Also, an open cover next to it. This can also be seen in the beginning of the book with the crew on deck.

Shipyard in the background where many of these Russian boats come from.

Nice starboard quarter shot

Circular access plate visible in the hull. Maintenance of the rear planes was high as the hydraulics often froze in place.

Even in the clutter of decommissioning, the Alfa shows graceful lines.

Another view of the row of cylinders just below the skin of the deck.

View of cylinders from starboard.

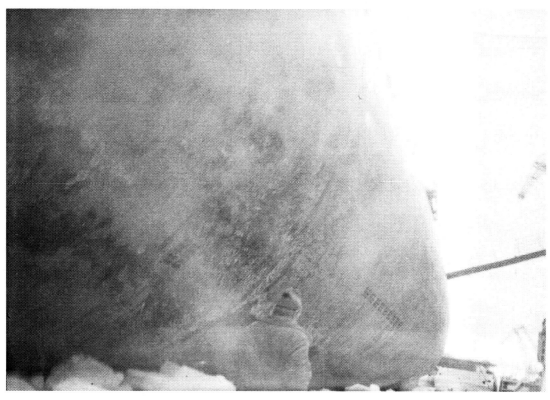

Some below the waterline details. A row of flood grates is seen.

Reactor seawater intake.

Intake grill for sea water cooling of the reactor. In a departure from other navies, Russians accept the trade off of increased water drag for less pump noise to move the water with these scoops.

Here is a drawing showing the intake and outlet path for the reactor cooling.
The creeper motor is shown also.

Here are the coolant outlets.

Clean view of the lower stern area. Some screw detail is evident also.

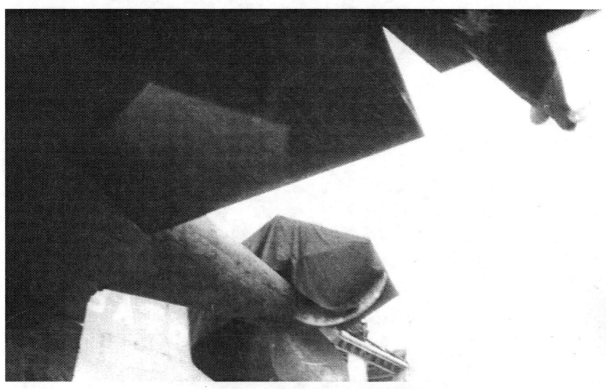

Access cover for creeper motor maintenance can be seen here.
The main screw was handmade solid titanium.

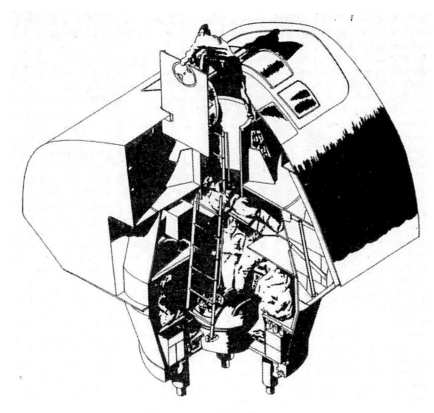

Escape module diagram

Alfa escape module.

Module on display found on all the modern Russian nuclear submarines.
On one occasion one was used with partial success.
It was the Komsomolets. It did save a life from the depths.

Windscreen in the up position. Likely, this is used for a trainer.

A sectioned Alfa hull with the torpedo tubes still there. Possibly remnant of K64. K64 had a reactor freeze and was cut in half and used for a trainer.

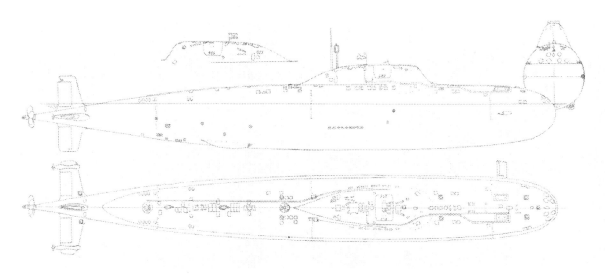

АПЛ К-64 пр.705 на государственных испытаниях в Белом море. Декабрь 1971 г.

K64. The first Alfa.

The multipurpose Akula 971

Akula is the Russian name for shark. The Akula designation sometimes causes confusion
with the Typhoon. Typhoon is another NATO designation for the 941 project.
The confusion comes in because the Russians call it their Akula class.

Sleek in design, the Akula is much quieter than her predecessors.
White horizontal markings are "parade dress". Often later removed, it also marks the passive
hull sensor locations so tug operators will not press there.

The Vepr, a later generation Akula just before the Gepard.
The Vepr had the characteristic pod on the upper rudder for the towed array. With the Gepard, this has been changed to a much smaller design. This was because the hydrodynamic properties of the classic Akula pod at low speed tend to pull the trailing line into the screw.

A sailor enjoying the peace of fishing.

These three rocks are well known to Russian submariners as they come to home port.

Securing topside for sea.

The raised, arched slot in the deck actually is the center of fold open doors to deploy a communications buoy that is torpedo shaped. After the doors close, the tether passes through that slot. The buoy goes to the surface while the submarine stays below undetected.

Pier side

Scanning the horizon with the microphone in hand to alert the command center.

Underway with the mast array raised.

Cockpit details of the Pantera

Looking back from the Pantera cockpit.

SOKS Sensor array (Sistema Obnaruzheniya Kilwaternogo Selda)
or wake detection system, on the leading edge of the Akula

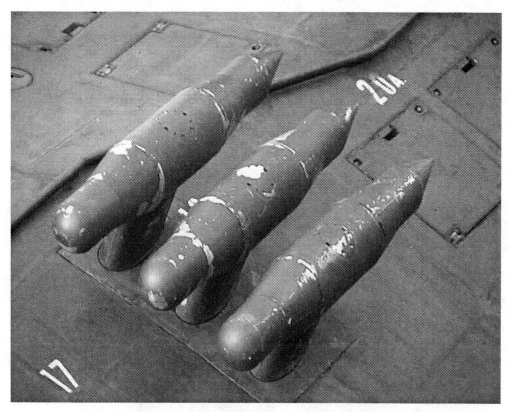

Hull mounted sensors found on later Akulas. Safety track in the background.

More detail toward the aft end of the sail.

Commander in the control room.

An Akula under construction.
It is rare to see the shutter doors open for the torpedoes

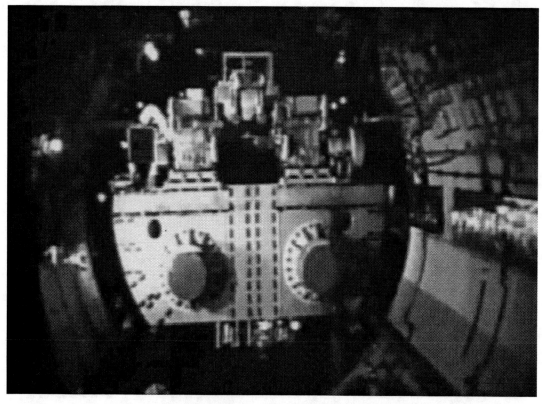

The nuclear reactor assembly being inserted into the hull during construction.

Insulator for isolating the interior machinery and crew from outside noise. This method is called "rafting".

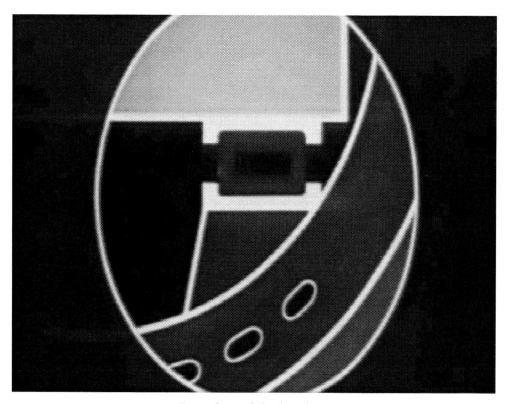

Location of the insulator

Seawater intake on an early Akula. Later variants would have a sleeker, "shark fin" shape.

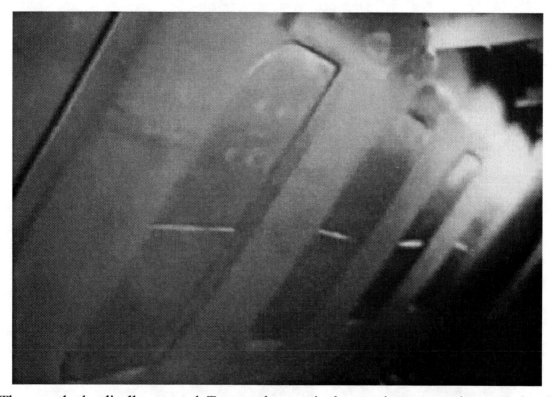

These are hydraulically operated. Two can be seen in the top picture over the man's head. They control how fast water is allowed in the boat.

The screw of the Akula, clearly showing the attenuator shown in the earlier chapter about the Alfa. This was a source of controversy years back due to the sale of some milling machinery and the Johnny Walker spy ring.

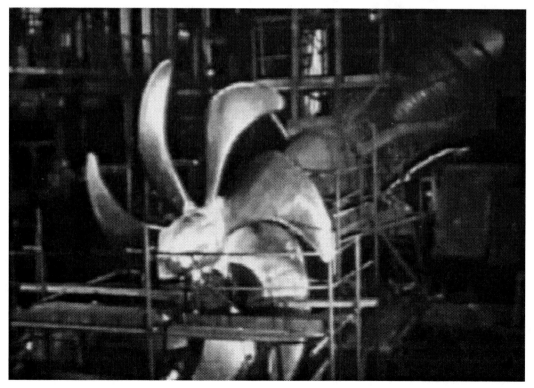

Another view

The communications pod partially exposed.

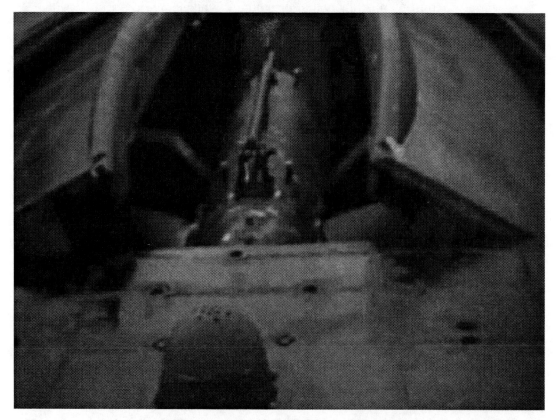

Here, one can better see the antenna on the pod that flips forward when deployed.

The communications pod, shown here, is rising up out of its bay.

In this drawing, the pod is shown fully deployed.

Locations of active and passive sonar systems

Baffling pattern inside the seawater intake system for cooling.

Characteristic of Russian design, the creeper motors are a feature of the Akula also.
One major difference is they are concealed just behind the intakes
and swing into position when needed.

Shown in this drawing in the deployed position.
Be certain they are used for stealth.

A command view.

Return to base. The Soviet era style block housing for the naval personnel clearly seen.

Nice angle of location of SOKS sensors on the top of the sail.
Visible here is a group of similar sensors on the stub fin standing on the hull.

Escort to port

Returning from the Barents Sea

Sitting much lower in the water.
The Russian submarines have much higher reserve buoyancy with the double hull design.

The Tiger
The hull color is darker on this submarine. Possibly an experiment in paint.
In history, the Russians tried many different paint schemes. The Alfa, for example was known to
have three lower hull colors. Black, Anti-foul green, and, the most accepted primer color.
To my knowledge, all of the 971 class boats had primer color lower paint.

Snow and ice on the deck of a departing Akula.
A reminder of the harsh conditions nature put on men and machine.

Like artwork.

The Akula screw.

Much more attention is given to machining and design to increase quietness.

Attenuator or flat blades on the hub are to thwart wake homing torpedoes.

The silver caps on the base of the blades are anodes that sacrifice themselves to save the screw when using dissimilar metals in the salt water.

This particular screw shown is from an early boat.

Attenuators are common on later Russian submarines.

The Alfa was the last to have hand made screws. The screw on the Alfa was also titanium.

To quote an Alfa officer, "They were very precious to us".

Navigation from the cockpit

Hello from the boys of Severodvinsk

Outline of the escape module is visible

The classic Ushanka hat of the Russian.
With the appropriate badge, approved headwear of officers

Here we begin a slow front to back view for detail

Bow emergency marker buoy.
Also, a slight change in pattern in the hull plates in the center.
This goes down the side of the hull and is a passive sensor section.

51

Sail faring into the hull proper.
This version does not have many of the hull sensors that stand off.

Again, the escape pod outline is visible.
Just behind that, in the open position, is the navigation light.
On the Alfa class, these navigation lights were opened
by hand by lowering someone down the side of the sail.

Here is where the communication buoy is housed

The recognizable towed array pod.
When first seen on a Russian submarine, western sources were worried about a
new propulsion system. This design is done away with the Gepard.
So new and different an Akula, it is almost a new class.

The next few photographs will show different emblems on some of the submarines. Since the passing of the Soviet Union, more and more are seen on the sides of the different classes, much like the American World War II bombers.

SOKS sensors also seen.

This photograph was made when the Russia was the Soviet Union.
The red star and hammer and sickle have been replaced with the Russian flag as seen below

Typical badge placement

An early Akula model.
It is normal practice to place a badge on the bow on commissioning.

In the frigid waters of Murmansk.
Note the floating docks attached.
These move with the boat to different work areas.

In dry dock.
Many features are visible.
The lower sensor similar to the one on top of the hull.
The lighter shade of the side hull passive sensors above and
below the painted section so tugs will not push there.
Also evident is the newer style, shark fin intake

At the famous shipyard, Sevorodvinsk. In the building in the background is the only location large enough to build the Typhoon.

A poor resolution, yet none the less outstanding photograph.

As with the Alfa, the Akula has a front hatch low in the front of the sail.
Also, there is a power port connection in the side of the sail itself shown here.

Some maintenance to the towed array pod.
Possibly reinstalling fresh trailing wire.

Removal of the escape pod for maintenance.

Damage aft of the escape module.
Perhaps this was the reason for inspection of the escape module.
But that is only speculation.

Not torpedo doors, it is where the decoys are released.
The center three doors opened are where the torpedoes are loaded.

Sitting under a protective cover to keep prying satellites from watching.
Creeper motor outline for the cover is behind the intake.

Looking forward reveals the below-the-waterline sensor.

Trim tabs on the stern planes.
This feature is also on the rudders

The Gepard

An evolution of the Akula, the Gepard is advanced enough to be called a fourth generation
submarine. The Akula II is a generation three. Many subtle differences exist between the two.
Although most observers only notice the much smaller pod at the top rudder.
In fact, there are many differences, including enhanced stealth.
A very minor change is the navigation lights are ahead of the escape module
instead of behind it, as in the other Akulas.

Better view of the most noticeable difference. The pod.

Another departure from the classic Akula for the Gepard. The sail.
While still definitely Russian shaped characteristics, it is shaped more like a western sail.
That is, not faired in at an angle on the side. SOKS array and other sensors bristle from the hull.
A marker light that is used for night navigation positioning is just ahead of the marker buoy.
Also, the Gepard has and extra hatch on the starboard side of the sail.
Handrails have been added to aid in skirting the sail in rough seas.
Of course, the safety track down both sides is a carry over from earlier designs.

Here, the module is being readied for removal and maintenance.

Loading of weapons on the Gepard for a patrol.

Gepard backing out of the construction hall

On the lower hull, behind the intakes about half way back to the rudder,
discharge outlets seem to be placed. Two rectangular boxes can be seen.
Again speculation, but plausible.

Another good detail view.
Lighter colors on the lower hull again indicate locations of passive listening systems.
Between the lower chin and the lighter side panel, at the midline, it where the bow planes extend
from. They extend straight out, and retract the same. Unlike the Typhoon, which does swing out
ninety degrees and locks into place.

Full starboard profile
Four sensors can be seen projecting from the hull at the four o'clock position

Note Russian markings on the building hall.

Cyrillic roughly translates to "Good luck Gepard"

Final view of the Gepard.
A remarkable machine indeed.

Leviathan of the Deep
Typhoon 941

Presenting the world's largest submarine.
Due to political reasons, the number of Typhoons has been reduced to three instead of six.
Of the remaining three, they are being upgraded with new electronics and missile capabilities
and should remain in service for several more years until the next class is fully operational.
The same is true of the sister to the Typhoon, the Delta IV.
Unique to the Typhoon is the placement of the missiles forward of the sail.
The Typhoon also has the escape modules which have the capacity to rescue the entire crew.
There are two modules. Each located on the bulge on the main hull on either side of the sail.

Impressive bow wave is due to two OK 650 reactors pushing that
enormous mass through the water.

Seen here as the crew stows the lines for sea, a Typhoon goes on patrol.
Details seen here include the rear hatch just ahead of the rudder.
The short stub fin to the left of the hatch is retractable and has to do with flow to the twin screws.

The two sailors on the deck are standing on one of the escape modules.
The outline of the module can be seen if one looks closely.

Here in the center front, one can see the three elongated hatches for loading torpedoes,
including the Shkval, a rocket powered torpedo capable of 200 miles per hour underwater.
Just below the loading hatches, the top two torpedo doors are visible.

Navigating the passage home.

Looking back down the two safety tracks toward the stern, a definite lean
can be seen as the boat commands a powered turn.

A refitted Typhoon.
Note the "Parade Dress" of white lines indicating normal waterline on the hull and shrouds. Also, the rear stub rudder show raised in an earlier photograph is retracted, as are the top side intakes. Top of the upper rudder is changed also from earlier variants.

The emergency marker buoy seen to the starboard side rear of the sail.

A commanding presence

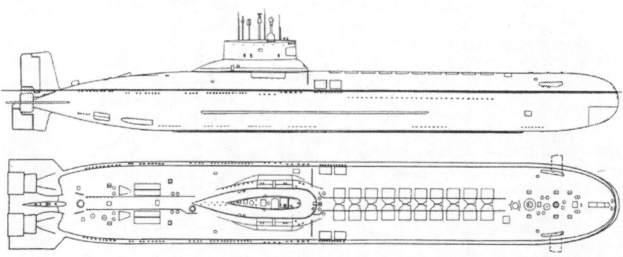

General configuration of a Typhoon.

Navigation from the cockpit.
The mast to the left of the sailor, and just behind the officer, are flag masts.

Here the boat is running "deck awash",
or just even with the surface for the main hull.

Looking back from the bow.

Here a Typhoon is passing a jetty to open sea.

Typhoon raising the periscope.
This image is a still from a video. That causes some loss of resolution.

Navigation lights can be seen here at the head of the sail, and on the side.
As with the windows, they are outlined in white "parade dress".

Massive size of the stern is evident when compared to the man standing there.

Small joysticks control the enormous stern surfaces.

Tape drive computer system.

Attenuator on screw hub once again, are evident.
The horizontal plate on the top and bottom of the lower rudder aid in turning.
Those plates are also on the stern planes

To the right side of the picture, in effect, says
"USA will not pass". This was taken in 1983.

This was taken in 2002 during a refit.

An older, but outstanding dry dock photograph.

These two photographs also came from videos.

Mammoth size is clear.
Reactor intakes can be seen through the girder.

What looks to be a trim tab at the base of the rudder is actually fixed.

Partially hidden from overhead intelligence satellites.

Draft markings located on the sail can be seen.

Aft details

Up close and personal view of the attenuator on a Typhoon screw.

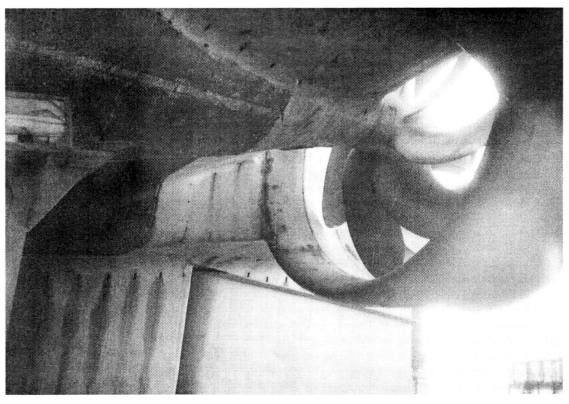

The blades of the screw itself.

Looking down the port side from the lower stern section.
The reactor cooling intake can be seen.

The same view from slightly different angle.

Simple grate design seen here just above the icy cold waters.

Upper rudder view again.
Note also the hull is shaped to guide the water into the shroud.

The lighter band seen on the hull is weathering.
Here the boat is sitting a little higher than before.

Bow in the cold waters

Detail of bow plane doors.

Typhoon number TK208 showing the vertical three pair arrangement of the torpedo doors
and the unusual shape

A small piece of the acoustic tile is missing here just above the starboard upper torpedo door.
A smaller one is also seen missing above the port side, as well.
Acoustic tiles are common on almost all submarines worldwide. It aids in being undetectable.
The Alfa actually had acoustic deadener on the inside of the easy case instead of the outside.

A prototype testing hull used in the design of the project 941.
It is unconfirmed this model has been moved to Moscow to be in a museum.

The purpose of a Typhoon in action.

The business end.

The tugs are welcome help in maneuvering in harbor for this large a boat.

The Typhoon can carry out its mission from pier side now with improved weapons systems.
The only reason to put to sea now is to remain untouchable by stealth.

Typhoon tied to a floating moor.

Artic sunset.

The Beluga project 1710
The Russian Albacore

The Beluga in Sevastopol Ukraine.
A unique submarine. Experimental in nature, the Beluga sported a body of revolution design hull with a 1 in 7 ideal aspect ratio. As with the American Albacore, the Beluga was intended to be used as a test bed of design. It was unarmed as it was for scientific study only. Research performed tested hull shape in the water, and with some success, tested submerged polymer emulsion to decrease drag on the skin. Using some common parts to other submarines, the Beluga used the same periscope and radar, Type MPK-50 "Kaskad", as the Kilo. It was not equipped with a snorkel for the diesel.
Often seen in the port of Sevastopol. The project 1710 also used the nearby base in the secret city of Balaclava. Since decommissioned after the change of politics in Russia. Even the former secret port of Balaclava is now accessible to the public. Balaclava today has the feel of a Mediterranean port, with excellent seafood. I recommend it.

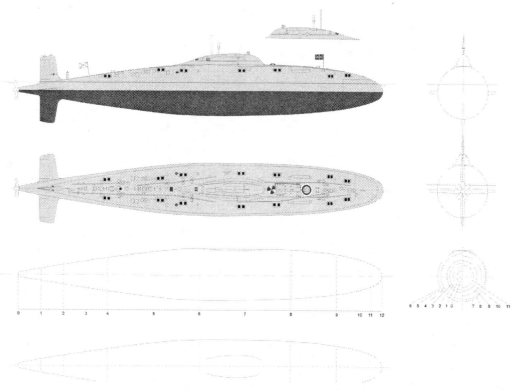

Beluga plans and sectionals.

Seen here with part of the Russian Black Sea Fleet.

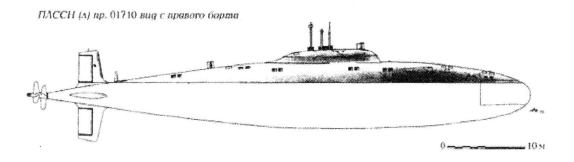

ПАССН (л) пр. 01710 вид с правого борта

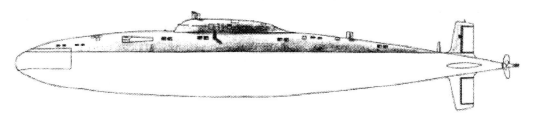

ПАССН (л) пр. 01710 вид с левого борта

Отличаются винтами, очевидно, указаны испытываемые типы винтов

There are no pictures of the Beluga's bow planes.
But the location is indicated here as ahead of the sail on the upper hull,
similar to the Victor class.

Here, in Inkerman near Sevastopol, the Beluga awaits decommissioning.
Sensors for measurement were all over the hull.
Note on standing on the stub foil at the front of the sail.

The author recognizes this as Balaclava Harbor.
This was home of operations and testing of the Beluga during the Soviet Union's rule.

Remnants of a castle wall on the east side of Balaclava harbor.
This photograph was taken at the entrance to the submarine pen under the mountain.
At one time, this harbor was all about submarines and the base under the mountain could house
five thousand people. There was also a special room for storage of nuclear weapons.
Beluga in the background.

Pier side at Balaclava.
When this picture was taken, Balaclava was not even admitted to exist to the civilian population
of Sevastopol forty-five minutes drive away.

Graceful, streamlined form evident here.

Sevastopol harbor.
Tied up next to another Russian submarine.

Just ahead of the rudder, a foil shaped mast stands holding another sensor.
Many sensors were placed away from the hull, to provide cleaner test results.

Here, the submarine is facing west in Sevastopol harbor.
Forward hatch and marker buoy clearly seen.

The later years…
Rust at the base of the sail. The short lived life of the Beluga begins to close.

Looking like something out of Star Wars.
Actually, it is a measurement sensor.

Bow shot showing off the clean lines.

Three hatches shown.
The front hatch is very long. Then the rear two appear more conventional.
The world's only known Russian pump jet submarine, a Kilo, is in the background.

Stern view.

Port sail side.
Bizarre sensor location seen

Another bow to stern photograph.

Interior photographs of the Beluga just prior to being scrapped in Inkerman.

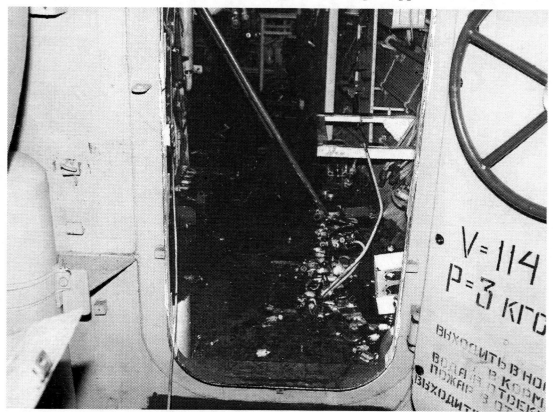

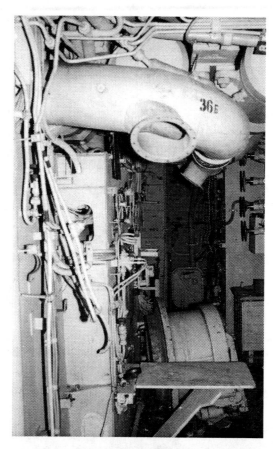

Looking inside from the sail area.

Sail, masts, interior removed. Little remains of the once unique submarine.
Note screw can be seen well now that the hull sits higher in the water.

Here, just prior to the mast removal.
Even a hatch where the sail used to be is visible.

Look for new releases from Cardinal Productions in the near future about Russian submarines on books and DVD.

A Cardinal Enterprise Release